To Be a Friend

To Be a Friend

Sayings and Verses
Celebrating the Beauty of Friendship

Edited by Edward Lewis and Robert Myers

Illustrated by Carolyn Jones

HALLMARK EDITIONS

To Be a Friend

The first foundation of friendship is not the power of conferring benefits, but the equality with which they are received, and may be returned.   *Funius*

All like the purchase; few the price will pay;
And this makes friends such miracles to-day.
                    Edward Young

Think of the importance of friendship in the education of men. It will make a man honest; it will make him a hero; it will make him a saint. It is the state of the just dealing with the just, the magnanimous with the magnanimous, the sincere with the sincere, man with man.
                    Thoreau

WHO IS MY FRIEND?

A certain man was going down from Jerusalem to Jericho; and he fell among robbers, which both stripped him and beat him, and departed, leaving him half dead. And by chance a certain priest was going down that way: and when he saw him, he passed by on the other side. But a certain Samaritan, as he journeyed, came where he was: and when he saw him, he was moved with compassion, and came to him, and bound up his wounds, pouring on them oil and wine; and he set him on his own beast, and brought him to an inn, and took care of him. And on the morrow he took out two pence, and gave them to the host, and said, Take care of him; and whatsoever thou spendest more, I, when I come back again, will repay thee. Which of these . . . , thinkest thou, proved neighbor unto him that fell among the robbers?

From the Gospel of St. Luke

I often find myself going back to Darwin's saying about the duration of a man's friendship being one of the best measures of his worth.   *Anne Thackeray Ritchie*

We never know the true value of friends. While they live we are too sensitive of their faults: when we have lost them we only see their virtues.   *J. C. and A. W. Hare*

What a thing friendship is—
World without end!   *Robert Browning*

The comfort of having a friend may be taken away, but not that of having had one.
                                                        Seneca

Friends are the Ancient and Honorable of the earth. The oldest men did not begin friendship. It is older than Hindustan and the Chinese Empire. How long it has been cultivated, and still it is the staple article! It is a divine league forever struck.   *Thoreau*

I shun a friend who pronounces my actions to be good though they are bad. I like a simple friend, who holds my faults like a looking-glass before my face.   *Ghozali*

Friendship renders prosperity more brilliant, while it lightens adversity by sharing it and making its burden common. *Cicero*

If you have one true friend you have more than your share. *Thomas Fuller*

When two friends part they should lock up each other's secrets and exchange keys. The truly noble mind has no resentments.
Diogenes

It is a good and safe rule to sojourn in every place as if you meant to spend your life there, never omitting an opportunity of doing a kindness, or speaking a true word, or making a friend. *John Ruskin*

The best that we find in our travels is an honest friend. He is a fortunate voyager who finds many. *Robert Louis Stevenson*

Ceremony and great professing render friendship as much suspected as it does religion.
William Wycherly

He who throws away a friend is as bad as he who throws away his life. *Sophocles*

A crowd is not a company, and faces are but a gallery of pictures, and talk but a tinkling cymbal, where there is no love.   *Francis Bacon*

My friend is not perfect—nor am I—and so we suit each other admirably.   *Alexander Pope*

The more we love, the better we are; and the greater our friendships are, the dearer we are to God.   *Jeremy Taylor*

Behold, how good and how pleasant it is for brethren to dwell together in unity!
Psalm 133

God save me from my friends; I can take care of my enemies.   *English Proverb*

Of our mixed life two quests are given control;
Food for the body, friendship for the soul.

Arthur Upson

Without reciprocal mildness and temperance
there can be no continuance of friendship.
Every man will have something to do for his
friend, and something to bear with in him.

Owen Felltham

Friendship is immeasurably better than kindness.

Cicero

To have joy one must share it,—
Happiness was born a twin.   *Lord Byron*

Friendship is an education. It draws the friend
out of himself and all that is selfish and ig-
noble in him and leads him to life's higher
levels of altruism and sacrifice. Many a man
has been saved from a life of frivolity and emp-
tiness to a career of noble service by finding at
a critical hour the right kind of friend.

G. D. Prentice

To preserve a friend, three things are required:
to honor him present, praise him absent, and
assist him in his necessities.   *Italian Proverb*

12

There are no rules for friendship. It must be left to itself. We cannot force it any more than love. *William Hazlitt*

It is better to be in chains with friends than in a garden with strangers. *Persian Proverb*

An open foe may prove a curse,
But a pretended friend is worse. *John Gay*

However rare true love is, true friendship is rarer. *La Rochefoucauld*

What do we live for, if it is not to make life less difficult to others? *George Eliot*

We are the weakest of spendthrifts if we let one friend drop off through inattention, or let one push away another, or if we hold aloof from one for petty jealousy or heedless roughness. Would you throw away a diamond because it pricked you? One good friend is not to be weighed against all the jewels of the earth. *Will Carleton*

True happiness
Consists not in the multitude of friends,
But in their worth and choice. *Ben Jonson*

To thine own self be true,
And it must follow, as the night the day,
Thou canst not then be false to any man.

Shakespeare

He is my friend! The words
Brought Summer and the birds;
And all my Winter time
Thawed into running rhyme
And rippled into song,
Warm, tender, brave and strong.

And so it sings to-day—
So may it sing alway!
Let each mute measure end
With "Still he is my friend."

James Whitcomb Riley

We just shake hands at meeting
With many that come nigh;
We nod the head in greeting
To many that go by.
But welcome through the gateway
Our few old friends and true;
Then hearts leap up and straightway
There's open house for you,—
Old friends,
There's open house for you! *Gerald Massey*

ALL LOSSES RESTORED

When to the sessions of sweet silent thought
I summon up remembrance of things past,
I sigh the lack of many a thing I sought,
And with old woes new wail my dear
    time's waste:
Then can I drown an eye, unused to flow,
For precious friends hid in death's
    dateless night,
And weep afresh love's long since
    cancell'd woe,
And moan the expense of many a
    vanish'd sight:
Then can I grieve at grievances foregone,
And heavily from woe to woe tell o'er
The sad account of fore-bemoaned moan,
Which I new pay as if not paid before.
But if the while I think on thee, dear friend,
All losses are restored and sorrows end.

Shakespeare

He is no friend who in thine hour of pride
Brags of his love and calls himself thy kin.
He is a friend who hales his fellow in,
And clangs the door upon the wolf outside.

Sa'di (tr. Sir Ed. Arnold)

If instead of a gem, or even a flower, we should cast the gift of rich thought into the heart of a friend, that would be giving as the angels give.

George MacDonald

Keep not ill company lest you increase the number.

George Herbert

That man may last, but never lives,
Who much receives but nothing gives;
Whom none can love, whom none can thank,
Creation's blot, creation's blank.

Thomas Gibbons

It is only the great-hearted who can be true friends; the mean and the cowardly can never know what true friendship is.

Charles Kingsley

I know not whether our names will be immortal; I am sure our friendship will.

Walter Savage Landor

If a man could mount to Heaven and survey the mighty universe, his admiration of its beauties would be much diminished unless he had someone to share in his pleasure.

Cicero

Those friends thou hast, and their
    adoption tried,
Grapple them to thy soul with hoops of steel,
But do not dull thy palm with entertainment
Of each new hatched, unfledged comrade.

Shakespeare

Nothing is so dangerous as an ignorant friend:
a wise enemy is much better.

Jean De La Fontaine

True friends, like ivy and the wall
Both stand together, and together fall.

Thomas Carlyle

It is not enough to love those who are near and dear to us. We must show them that we do so.

Lord Avebury

A man is judged by his friends, for the wise and foolish have never agreed.

Baltasar Gracian

If words came as readily as ideas and ideas as
feeling, I could say ten hundred kindly things.
You know my supreme happiness at having
one on earth whom I can call a friend.

Charles Lamb

I am not of that feather to shake off
My friend when he must need me.

Shakespeare

The language of friendship is not words, but
meanings. It is an intelligence above language.

Thoreau

Every man should have a fair-sized cemetery
in which to bury the faults of his friends.

Henry Ward Beecher

How sweet, how passing sweet is solitude!
But grant me still a friend in my retreat,
Whom I may whisper—"Solitude is sweet."
La Bruyere

This is my friend, through good or ill report,
My friend. He who injures him by word
    or deed,
Were it but the thin film of an idle breath
Clouding the clear glass of a stainless soul,
He injures me. *Richard Hovey*

Friendship—our friendship—is like the
    beautiful shadows of evening,
Spreading and growing till life and its
    light pass away. *Michael Vitkovics*

There is a destiny which makes us brothers,—
None goes on his way alone;
All that we send into the lives of others,
Comes back into our own.

Edwin Markham

There is no desert like being friendless.
Baltasar Gracian

Fellowship in joy, not sympathy in sorrow, is
what makes friends. *Nietzsche*

Friendship, gift of Heaven, delight of great souls; friendship, which kings, so distinguished for ingratitude, are unhappy enough not to know. *Voltaire*

Friendship is the allay of our sorrows, the ease of our passions, the discharge of our oppressions, the sanctuary to our calamities, the counsellor of our thoughts, the exercise and improvement of what we meditate.

Jeremy Taylor

I find friendship to be like wine, raw when new, ripened with age, the true old man's milk and restorative cordial.

Thomas Jefferson

We do not wish for friends to feed and clothe our bodies,—neighbors are kind enough for that—but to do the like office to our spirits. For this few are rich enough, however well disposed they may be. *Thoreau*

When a friend asks there is no tomorrow.

George Herbert

I like a friend the better for having faults that one can talk about. *William Hazlitt*

Friendship cheers like a sunbeam; charms like a good story; inspires like a brave leader; binds like a golden chain; guides like a heavenly vision.   *Newell D. Hillis*

Friendships multiply joys, and divide griefs.
                                     H. G. Bohn

A true test of friendship,—to sit or walk with a friend for an hour in perfect silence without wearying of one another's company.
                           Dinah Mulock Craik

How can we tell what coming people are aboard the ships that may be sailing to us now from the unknown seas?   *Charles Dickens*

If a man find a prudent companion who walks with him, is wise, and lives soberly, he may walk with him, overcoming all dangers, happy, but considerate.   *The Buddha*

Who seeks a faultless friend rests friendless.
                              Turkish Proverb

Love Him, and keep Him for thy Friend, who, when all go away, will not forsake thee, nor suffer thee to perish at the last.
                              Thomas A Kempis

Nothing makes the earth seem so spacious as to have friends at a distance: they make the latitudes and longitudes.   *Thoreau*

TRUE FRIENDSHIP

'Tis hard to find in life
A friend, a bow, a wife,
Strong, supple to endure,
In stock and sinew pure,
In time of danger sure.

False friends are common. Yes, but where
True nature links a friendly pair,
The blessing is as rich as rare.

To bitter ends
You trust true friends,
Not wife nor mother,
Not son nor brother.

No long experience alloys
True friendship's sweet and supple joys;
No evil men can steal the treasure;
'Tis death, death only, sets a measure.

From the Panchatantra
(tr. A. W. Ryder)

It is well that there is no one without a fault, for he would not have a friend in the world.
William Hazlitt

That friendship will not continue to the end that is begun for an end.   *Francis Quarles*

There are three friendships which are advantageous, and three which are injurious. Friendship with the upright; friendship with the sincere; and friendship with the man of much observation; these are advantageous. Friendship with the man of specious airs; friendship with the insinuatingly soft; and friendship with the glib-tongued; these are injurious.
Confucius

One of the most beautiful qualities of true friendship is to understand and to be understood.   *Seneca*

A friendless man is like a left hand without a right.   *Hebrew Proverb*

Time draweth wrinkles in a fair face, but addeth fresh colors to a fast friend, which neither heat, nor cold, nor misery, nor place, nor destiny, can alter or diminish.   *John Lyly*

The making of friends who are real friends, is the best token we have of a man's success in life.   *Edward Everett Hale*

A faithful friend is a strong defence; and he that hath found such a one hath found a treasure. Nothing doth countervail a faithful friend, and his excellency is invaluable.   *Proverbs*

The ring of coin is often the knell of friendship.
                    La Rochefoucauld

Friendship that flows from the heart cannot be frozen by adversity, as the water that flows from the spring cannot congeal in winter.
                James Fenimore Cooper

Make not thy friend too cheap to thee, nor thyself too dear to him.   *James Howell*

I desire so to conduct the affairs of this administration that if at the end, when I come to lay down the reins of power, I have lost every other friend on earth, I shall at least have one friend left, and that friend shall be down inside of me.   *Abraham Lincoln*

Life is nothing without friendship.   *Cicero*

The greatest happiness of life is the conviction that we are loved, loved for ourselves, or rather loved in spite of ourselves.   *Victor Hugo*

If thou findest a good man, rise up early in the morning to go to him, and let thy feet wear the steps of his door.

The Apocryphal Book of Ecclesiasticus

God never loved me in so sweet a way before.
'Tis He alone who can such blessings send.
And when His love would new
   expressions find,
He brought thee to me and He said—
  "Behold a friend."   *Unknown*

The friend that faints is a foe.   *John Davies*

As gold more splendid from the fire appears,
Thus friendship brightens by the length
of years.   *Thomas Carlyle*

Men exist for the sake of one another.
Teach them, then, or bear with them.
                                    Marcus Aurelius

Friendship is a vase, which, when it is flawed
by heat, or violence, or accident, may as well
be broken at once; it can never be trusted
after. The more graceful and ornamental it
was, the more clearly do we discern the hope-
lessness of restoring it to its former state. Coarse
stones, if they are fractured, may be cemented
again; precious ones never.
                              Walter Savage Landor

He is my friend that succoreth me, not he that
pitieth me.   *Thomas Fuller*

We can never replace a friend. When a man
is fortunate enough to have several, he finds
they are all different. No one has a double in
friendship.   *Friedrich von Schiller*

Few there are that will endure a true friend.
                                        H. G. Bohn

We want but two or three friends, but these we cannot do without, and they serve us in every thought we think.   *Emerson*

You can hardly make a friend in a year, but you can lose one in an hour.
                                        Chinese Proverb

But, after all, the very best thing in good talk, and the thing that helps most, is friendship. How it dissolves the barriers that divide us, and loosens all constraint, and diffuses itself like some fine old cordial through all the veins of life—this feeling that we understand and trust each other, and wish each other heartily well! Everything into which it really comes is good.
                                        Henry Van Dyke

Instead of herds of oxen, endeavor to assemble flocks of friends about your house.   *Epictetus*

For believe me, in this world, which is ever slipping from under our feet, it is the pre-rogative of friendship to grow old with one's friends.   *Arthur S. Hardy*

A friend's frown is better than a fool's smile.
                                        C. E. Locke

To make the world a friendly place
One must show it a friendly face.

James Whitcomb Riley

He that is thy friend indeed
He will help thee in thy need.

If thou sorrow, he will weep,
If thou wake, he cannot sleep,

Thus, of every grief in heart
He with thee doth bear a part.

These are certain signs to know
Faithful friend from flattering foe.

Richard Barnfield

It is my joy in life to find
At every turning of the road
The strong arms of a comrade kind
To help me onward with my load;
And since I have no gold to give,
And love alone must make amends,
My only prayer is, while I live—
God make me worthy of my friends.

F. D. Sherman

When adversities flow, then love ebbs; but
friendship standeth stiffly in storms.

John Lyly

THE MEMORY OF THE HEART

If stores of dry and learned lore we gain,
We keep them in the memory of the brain,
Names, things, and facts,—whate'er we
   knowledge call,—
There is the common ledger for them all;
And images on this cold surface traced
Make slight impression, and are soon effaced.

But we've a page, more glowing and
   more bright,
On which our friendship and our love
   to write;
That these may never from the soul depart,
We trust them to the memory of the heart.
There is no dimming, no effacement there;
Each new pulsation keeps the record clear;
Warm, golden letters all the tablet fill,
Nor lose their lustre till the heart
   stands still.

Daniel Webster

There are evergreen men and women in the world, praise be to God!—not many of them, but a few. The sun of our prosperity makes the green of their friendship no brighter, the frost of our adversity kills not the leaves of their affection.   *Jerome K. Jerome*

Reprove a friend in secret, but praise him before others.   *Leonardo Da Vinci*

Ointment and perfume rejoice the heart; so doth the sweetness of a man's friend that cometh of hearty counsel. Thine own friend and thy father's friend forsake not.   *Solomon*

If all the gold in the world were melted down into a solid cube it would be about the size of an eight-room house. If a man got possession of all that gold—billions of dollars worth, he could not buy a friend, character, peace of mind, clear conscience, or a sense of beauty.
                    Charles Banning

What joy is better than the news of friends?
                    Robert Browning

A brother may not be a friend, but a friend will always be a brother.   *Benjamin Franklin*

That friend who serves, and seeks for gain,
And follows but for form,
Will pack when it begins to rain,
And leave you in the storm.   *Shakespeare*

We call that person who has lost his father, an
orphan; and a widower, that man who has
lost his wife. And that man who has known
that immense unhappiness of losing a friend,
by what name do we call him? Here every
human language holds its peace in impotence.
                                            Joseph Rioux

When Zeno was asked what a friend was, he
replied, "Another I."   *Diogenes*

There is no friend like the old friend who
    has shared our morning days,
No greeting like his welcome, no homage
    like his praise;
Fame is the scentless sunflower, with
    gaudy crown of gold;
But friendship is the breathing rose,
    with sweets in every fold.
                        Oliver Wendell Holmes

In prosperity it is very easy to find a friend;
in adversity, nothing is so difficult.   *Epictetus*

We do not make friends as we make houses, but discover them as we do the arbutus, under the leaves of our lives, concealed in our experience. *William Rader*

There is an idea abroad among moral people that they should make their neighbors good. One person I have to make good: myself. But my duty to my neighbor is much more nearly expressed by saying that I have to make him happy—if I may. *Robert Louis Stevenson*

The wise man will want to be ever with him who is better than himself. *Plato*

The vulgar estimate friends by the advantage to be derived from them. *Ovid*

The true friend seeks to give, not to take; to help, not to be helped; to minister, not to be ministered unto.   *William Rader*

If you have a friend worth loving,
Love him, yes, and let him know
That you love him ere life's evening
Tinge his brow with sunset glow;
Why should good words ne'er be said
Of a friend till he is dead?

                                    Thomas Hughes

To wail friends lost
Is not by much so wholesome—profitable,
As to rejoice at friends but newly found.

                                    Shakespeare

It is good to have some friends both in Heaven and Hell.   *George Herbert*

We know any friend chiefly by some form of manifestation in act. His inner life, as inner, is hidden from us as really as is the mind of God. And we have manifestations of God in like manner, and from them we may know directly his purpose and spirit . . . as we may know the purpose and spirit of our friend.

                                    Henry C. King

A friend that you have to buy won't be worth what you pay for him, no matter what that may be. *G. D. Prentice*

This matter of friendship is often regarded slightingly as a mere accessory of life, a happy chance if one falls into it, but not as entering into the substance of life. No mistake can be greater. It is, as Emerson says, not a thing of "glass threads or frost-work, but the solidest thing we know." *T. T. Munger*

I don't meddle with what my friends believe or reject, any more than I ask whether they are rich or poor; I love them.
James Russell Lowell

My friend is one whom I can associate with my choicest thoughts. *Thoreau*

In the hours of distress and misery, the eyes of every mortal man turn to friendship; in the hour of gladness and conviviality, what is our want? It is friendship. When the heart overflows with gratitude, or with any other sweet and sacred sentiment, what is the word to which it would give utterance? A friend.
Walter Savage Landor

Vex no man's secret soul—if that can be—
The path of life hath far too many a thorn!
Help whom thou may'st—for surely unto thee
Sharp need of help will e'er the end be borne.
Sa'di (tr. Sir Ed. Arnold)

Our chief want in life is somebody who shall make us do what we can. This is the service of a friend. *Emerson*

Fellowship is heaven, and lack of fellowship is hell; fellowship is life, and lack of fellowship is death; and the deeds that ye do upon earth, it is for fellowship's sake that ye do them.
William Morris

The friends of my friends are my friends.
Flemish Proverb

Judge before friendship,
then confide till death. *Young*

A man cannot speak to his son but as a father, to his wife but as a husband, to his enemy but upon terms; whereas a friend may speak as the case requires, and not as it sorteth with the person. *Francis Bacon*

Friendship is a word the very sight of which in print makes the heart warm.

Augustine Birrell

THE HEART'S ANCHOR

Think of me as your friend, I pray,
And call me by a loving name.
I will not care what others say,
If only you remain the same.
I will not care how dark the night,
I will not care how wild the storm,
Your love will fill my heart with light
And shield me close and keep me warm.

Think of me as your friend, I pray,
For else my life is little worth:
So shall your memory light my way,
Although we meet no more on earth.
For while I know your faith secure,
I ask no happier fate to see:
Thus to be loved by one so pure
Is honor rich enough for me.

William Winter

There is a magic in the memory of a schoolboy friendship; it softens the heart, and even affects the nervous system of those who have no heart.   *Benjamin Disraeli*

Friendship is like two clocks keeping time.
                                    Unknown

Let thy pity be a divining: to know first if thy friend wanteth pity. Perhaps he loveth in thee the unmoved eye, and the look of eternity.

Let thy pity for thy friend be hid under a hard shell; thou shalt bite out a tooth upon it. Thus will it have delicacy and sweetness.

Art thou pure air and solitude and bread and medicine to thy friend? Many a one cannot loosen his own fetters, but is nevertheless his friend's emancipator.

Art thou a slave? Then thou canst not be a friend. Art thou a tyrant? Then thou canst not have friends.   *Nietzche*

These things do not require to be spoken; there is something in the hand grip, and the look in the eye that makes you know your man.
                                C. H. Chambers

Never injure a friend, even in jest.   *Cicero*

Give me the avowed, the erect, the manly foe;
Bold I can meet, perhaps may turn his blow;
But of all plagues, good Heaven, thy
   wrath can send,
Save oh! save me from the Candid Friend.

George Channing

The bird a nest, the spider a web,
man friendship.
William Blake

Convey thy love to thy friend, as an arrow to
the mark, to stick there; not as a ball against
the wall to rebound back to thee.

Francis Quarles

There are three faithful friends—an old wife,
an old dog, and ready money.

Benjamin Franklin

I would not enter on my list of friends
(Though graced with polished manners
   and fine sense,
Yet wanting sensibility) the man
Who needlessly sets foot upon a worm.

William Cowper

How can life be true life without friends?
Ennius

A slender acquaintance with the world must convince every man that actions, not words, are the true criterion of the attachment of friends; and that the most liberal profession of good-will is very far from being the surest mark of it. *George Washington*

It is great to have friends when one is young, but indeed it is still more so when you are getting old. When we are young, friends are, like everything else, a matter of course. In the old days we know what it means to have them.
Edvard Grieg

Have no friends not equal to yourself.
Confucius

Give me one friend, just one, who meets
The needs of all my varying moods;
Be we in noisy city street,
Or in dear Nature's solitudes.

One who can let the World go by,
And suffer not a minute's pang:
Who'd dare to shock propriety
With me, and never care a hang.

One who can share my grief or mirth,
And know my days to praise or curse;
And rate me just for what I'm worth,
And find me still,—Oh, not so worse!

Give me one friend, for peace or war,
And I shall hold myself well blest,
And richly compensated for
The cussedness of all the rest.

Esther M. Clark

The condition which high friendship demands
is ability to do without it.

Ralph W. Emerson

Were I made to prognosticate the future of
man, I would first put my ear to his heart.

Alfred Henry Lewis

The friendship between you and me I will not compare to a chain; for that the rains might rust or the falling trees break.

George Bancroft

I never considered a difference of opinion in politics, in religion, in philosophy, as cause for withdrawing from a friend.

Thomas Jefferson

To oppress a suppliant, to kill a wife,
   to rob a *Brahman*, and to betray one's friend,
These are the four great crimes.

The Mahabharata

To keep a few friends, but these without capitulation—above all, on the same grim condition, to keep friends with himself—here is a task for all that a man has of fortitude and delicacy.   *Robert Louis Stevenson*

The very idea of a worthy friendship implies that the friends need and desire each other; are sure that each has much to give to the other; and so are continuously receptive and eager for the other's gift. Unteachableness shuts one off from his friend's best gift.

Henry Churchill King

For thus the royal mandate ran
When first the human race began:
The social, friendly, honest man,
    Whate'er he be,
'Tis he fulfills great nature's plan,
    And none but he.   *Robert Burns*

O friend, my bosom said,
Through thee alone the sky is arched,
Through thee the rose is red,
All things through thee take nobler form,
And look beyond the earth,
The mill-round of our fate appears
A sun-path in thy worth.
Me, too, thy nobleness has taught
To master my despair;
The fountains of my hidden life
Are through thy friendship fair.
        Ralph Waldo Emerson

To distrust a friend is a double folly.
Trust *is* friendship.   *Bryant A. Wooster*

He who has a thousand friends,
Has not a friend to spare,
And he who has one enemy
Will meet him everywhere.
        Ali Ben Abu Taheb

THEY TOLD ME HERACLEITUS

They told me, Heracleitus, they told me
    you were dead;
They brought me bitter news to hear and
    bitter tears to shed.
I wept as I remembered how often you and I
Had tired the sun with talking, and
    sent him down the sky.

And now that thou art lying, my dear old
    Carian guest,
A handful of gray ashes long, long ago
    at rest,
Still are thy pleasant voices, thy
    nightingales awake,
For Death he taketh all away, but
    these he cannot take.

Callimachus

People who have warm friends are healthier and happier than those who have none. A single real friend is a treasure worth more than gold or precious stones. Money can buy many things, good and evil. All the wealth of the world could not buy you a friend or pay you for the loss of one.   *C. D. Prentice*

Friendship's the wine of life.

Edward Young

It is good to give a stranger a meal, or a night's lodging. It is better to be hospitable to his good meaning and thought, and give courage to a companion. We must be as courteous to a man as we are to a picture, which we are willing to give the advantage of a good light.   *Emerson*

A wise man gets more out of his enemies than a fool gets out of his friends.

Baltasar Gracian

It is worse to mistrust a friend then to be deceived by him.   *French Proverb*

Friends are the thermometers by which we may judge the temperature of our fortunes.

Countess of Blessington

It is chance that makes brothers, but hearts
that make friends. *E. von Geibel*

I hear it was charged against me that I
   sought to destroy institutions,
But really I am neither for nor against
   institutions,
Only I will establish in Manahatta and in
   every city of these States, inland and
   seaboard,
And in the fields and woods, and above
   every keel little or large that dents
   the water,
The institution of the dear love of comrades.
Walt Whitman

The only reward of virtue, is virtue: The only
way to have a friend is to be one. *Emerson*

Be true to your word, your work,
and your friend. *Thoreau*

He that ceaseth to be a friend never was a good
one. *H. G. Bohn*

Friendship maketh daylight in the understand-
ing, out of darkness and confusion of thoughts.
Francis Bacon

Few men have strength to honor a friend's success without envy.   *Aeschylus*

Happy is the house that shelters a friend.

Emerson

I find as I grow older that I love those most whom I loved first.   *Thomas Jefferson*

Life without a friend is death without a witness.   *George Herbert*

Who keep company with the wolf learn to howl.   *Thomas Fuller*

Friendship above all ties does bind the heart,
And faith in friendship is the noblest part.

Lord Orrery

My friend peers in on me with merry
Wise face, and though the sky stay dim,
The very light of day, the very
Sun's self comes in with him.   *Swinburne*

Love is a sudden blaze, which soon decays;
Friendship is like the sun's eternal rays;
Not daily benefits exhaust the flame;
It still is giving, and still burns the same.
                        John Gay

The name of friend is common, but faith in friendship is rare.   *Phaedrus*

There is no folly equal to that of throwing away friendship in a world where friendship is so rare.   *Edward Bulwer-Lytton*

Friendship is to be valued for what there is in it, not what can be gotten out of it. To seek friendship for its utility is as futile as to seek the end of a rainbow for its bag of gold. A true friend is always useful in the highest sense; but we should beware of thinking of our friends as brother members of a mutual bene-fit association, with its periodical demands and threats of suspension for non-payment of dues.
                        Trumbull

There can be no friendship where there is no freedom. Friendship loves a free air, and will not be penned up in straight and narrow enclosures. *William Penn*

I account it one of the greatest demonstrations of real friendship, that a friend can really endeavor to have his friend advanced in honor, in reputation, in the opinion of wit or learning, before himself. *Jeremy Taylor*

Happy is he whose friends were born before him. *John Ray*

All men have their frailties, and whoever looks for a friend without imperfections will never find what he seeks. *Robert Louis Stevenson*

I wonder if there is anything in this world as beautiful as good, strong friendship between two men. They don't go round doing the mollycoddle act; they don't kiss each other every time they meet; in fact, they never do kiss each other, unless one is lying cold in death, but they are sure one knows the other is always going to stand by him, and they feel that no matter what happens, each can rely on the other. *Wilbur D. Nesbit*

One ought still to honour the enemy in one's
friend. Canst thou go nigh unto thy friend,
and not go over him?   *Nietzsche*

Thou goest thy way and I go mine;
Apart, yet not afar;
Only a thin veil hangs between
The pathways where we are;
And "God keep watch 'tween thee and me,"
This is my prayer;
He looks thy way. He looketh mine.
And keeps us near.   *Julia A. Baker*

I was angry with my friend:
I told my wrath, my wrath did end.
I was angry with my foe:
I told it not, my wrath did grow.

                                 William Blake

Choose thy friends like thy books,
few but choice.   *James Howell*

No man can be happy without a friend, nor
be sure of his friend till he is unhappy.

Thomas Fuller

You may take sarza to open the liver; steel to
open the spleen; flowers of sulpher for the
lungs; castoreum for the brain; but no receipt
openeth the heart but a true friend, to whom
you may impart griefs, joys, fears, hopes, sus-
picions, counsels, and whatsoever lieth upon
the heart to oppress it, in a kind of civil shrift
or confession.   *Francis Bacon*

IN HASTE

From far, from eve and morning,
And yon twelve-winded sky,
The stuff to life to knit me
Blew hither; here am I.

Now—for a breath I tarry,
Nor yet disperse apart—
Take my hand quick and tell me,
What have you in your heart?

Speak now, and I will answer;
How shall I help you, say;
Ere to the wind's twelve quarters
I take my endless way?

A. E. Housman

Thy friend put in thy bosom; wear his eyes
Still in thy heart, that he may see what's there.

George Herbert

There is no better looking-glass than an old
friend. *Thomas Fuller*

Blessed are they who have the gift of making
friends, for it is one of God's best gifts. It in-
volves many things, but above all the power of
going out of one's self, and appreciating what
is noble and loving in another.

Thomas Hughes

Friends got without desert will be lost without
cause. *H. G. Bohn*

Choose a friend as thou dost a wife, till death
separate you. *William Penn*

Two are better than one; because they have
a good reward for their labor. For if they fall,
the one will lift up his fellow; but woe to him
that is alone when he falleth; for he hath not
another to help him up. And if one prevail
against him, two shall withstand him; and a
threefold cord is not quickly broken.

Old Testament

Friend is a word of Royal tone;
Friend is a Poem all alone.   *A Persian Poet*

Friendship always benefits.   *Seneca*

He who would grow into larger and richer
friendships must recognize first of all that, if
his friend is in truth worthy of such a friendship as he seeks, the great way is by personal
association. One cannot grab up and hurry off
with the fine fruits of friendship. No friendship that counts for much with either men or
God can become one's own without the giving
of time, of thought, of attention, of honest response.... No friendship is so high, so fine, or
so assured that it does not need that the friends
should take time to be together, that they
should be willing to think enough to enter with
some appreciation into the thought and experience of each other, and that they should
make honest response to the best in each
other's character and in each other's vision.
      Henry C. King

Strike hands with me, the glasses brim,
the sun is on the heather
And love is good and life is long and
two are best together.   *Edward Wrightman*

A man's growth is seen in the successive choirs of his friends. *Emerson*

Be a friend; the rest will follow. *Dickerson*

My friend should honor him who honors me. *Homer*

They only are true friends who think as one. *French Proverb*

He that goeth to bed with dogs ariseth with fleas. *John Sanford*

A true friend unbosoms freely, advises justly, assists readily, adventures boldly, takes all patiently, defends courageously, and continues a friend unchangeably. *William Penn*

No man is self-made who unmakes others.
Stephen Voris

Every true friend is a glimpse of God.
Lucy Larcom

Common friendships will admit of division;
one may love the beauty of this, the good
humor of that person, the liberality of a third,
the paternal affection of a fourth, the fraternal
love of a fifth, and so on. But this friendship
that possesses the whole soul, and there rules
and sways with an absolute sovereignty, can
admit of no rival.   *Montaigne*

Everyman's friend is everyman's fool.
Dutch Proverb

Nature produced us related to one another,
since she created us from the same source and
to the same end. She engendered in us mutual
affection and made us prone to friendships. . . .
Through her orders, our hands are ready to
help in the good work. Our relations with one
another are like a stone arch, which would
collapse if the stones did not mutually support
each other, and which is upheld in this very
way.   *Seneca*

A friend is worth all the hazards we can run.
Edward Young

An untried friend is like an uncracked nut.
Russian Proverb

And when the wintry tempest blows,
And January's sleets and snows
   Are spread o'er every vale and hill,
With one to tell a merry tale
O'er roasted nuts and humming ale,
   sit, and care not for the gale;—
      And let the world laugh, an' it will.
Luis De Gongora Y Argote
(tr. Longfellow)

Designed by Carole Muller

Set in Walbaum, a light open typeface designed by Justus Erich Walbaum (1768-1839), a type founder at Goslar and at Weimar.

Printed on Hallmark Eggshell Book paper.